MINDFULNESS AND MEDITATION FOR BEGINNERS

DISCOVER THE POWER OF MINDFUL THINKING FOR STRESS MANAGEMENT: WITH EXERCISES AND RELAXATION TECHNIQUES TO DECLUTTER YOUR MIND, REDUCE ANXIETY AND IMPROVE SLEEP

JEN CARTER

Copyright © 2025 by Hope Books Ltd

All rights reserved.

No part of this book may be reproduced in any form or by any electronic or mechanical means, including information storage and retrieval systems, without written permission from the author, except for the use of brief quotations in a book review.

This book is not intended as a substitute for the medical advice of physicians. The reader should regularly consult a physician in matters relating to his/her health and particularly with respect to any symptoms that may require diagnosis or medical attention.

Although the author and publisher have made every effort to ensure that the information in this book was correct at press time, the author and publisher do not assume and hereby disclaim any liability to any party for any loss, damage, or disruption caused by errors or omissions, whether such errors or omissions result from negligence, accident, or any other cause.

CONTENTS

1. Introduction — 1
2. What is Mindfulness? Why Meditate? — 5
3. The Problem with Our Lives — 13
4. The Health Benefits of Mindfulness and Meditation — 21
5. Practical Guide to Meditation Techniques — 29
6. A Guide to Mindfulness Techniques — 39
7. The Power of Mindfulness and Meditation — 53
8. Getting Started — 59
9. Conclusion — 67
10. One More Thing — 69
11. Mindfulness Meditations — 71

1

INTRODUCTION

If you've been curious the concepts of meditation and living a more mindful life, this book is the perfect introduction for you.

We'll dive into the concepts of mindfulness and meditation, and discover what these concepts mean for a better, healthier, and more enlightened lifestyle for you.

Our lives are so full of social media, high expectations, and the pressure to get ahead. It can be overwhelming and feel like we never have a moment to ourselves.

Many of us are simply on 'autopilot'. We get through our day and complete the motions of what is expected from us.

But how much time are we giving to ourselves? When do we pause to check in and see how we feel, ask ourselves how we are doing and how our physical and emotional health is?

Do we even take time to appreciate what is around us, or are we too consumed with our mind on other things?

So much of our life is spent thinking about the past or worrying about the future. It can be hard for us to live in and experience the present moment.

For many of us, we're busy multi-tasking and our brains are filled with many thoughts.

We could be having a conversation with someone but making dinner plans in our head. Perhaps we're in a meeting at work but struggling to focus as we're thinking about your personal life.

Sometimes we get through large portions of our day and can't even remember what we did!

Mindfulness is about leading a life where you are aware and present in the moment, at this exact time.

It's about experiencing your life, moment by moment. It's about living more fully.

Mindfulness urges us to be more present in our lives and be acutely aware of the situation we're in, and our surroundings.

Science has shown that there's health benefits to living a mindful life!

Mindfulness has been shown to reduce anxiety, depression, insomnia and blood pressure. It can even increase the quality of your personal relationships. Research studies have found that it can even help patients to better manage chronic pain.

Since the late 1960s and '70s, researchers in the United States have begun to study the effects of meditation. Their results only prove what societies around the world have known for thousands of years ago - meditation works!

Meditation is becoming a popular therapy, for those who make their physical and mental well-being a priority. Those individuals who are making time for meditation and mindfulness in their schedule are seeing the benefit.

For anyone new to mindfulness and meditation, you'll find a list of tips for getting started, that will help you begin to live a life that incorporates mindfulness and meditation into your busy day.

As with anything, your journey towards a mindful life, starts with a single step. You've already taken the first step, by reading this book. Let's find out how you can get started.

2

WHAT IS MINDFULNESS? WHY MEDITATE?

Mindfulness sounds like an easy enough concept - just pay attention to what you're doing and live in the moment, right?

In today's busy fast-paced life, finding time for anything, is something millions of people struggle with .

Have you ever sat down in your morning meeting at work, then when it's over you realize you remember nothing? Or how about if you got in the car for a long car ride and you can't even remember the journey to get to your destination?

You may even have been too busy thinking of the plans you have to fulfil, and the people you have to meet, that you didn't even stop to look at the view around you.

For many people, that's their normal life. But *you* can change things, *one simple step at a time.*

Mindfulness is about having your complete mind paying attention to exactly what you're doing now and what is happening in the moment.

You don't want to be agonizing about the future and its potential problems, or mulling over regrets about the past and the demons haunting you.

It's about right now! *This* moment!

Often, our minds aren't focusing on what we're doing right now. We're too busy thinking about something else and live with dividing our attention, even when we should be concentrating on one person or task.

In today's society, with smartphones and social media, it's hard to feel like you're fully appreciating every second. We are so consumed by what's happening elsewhere, we can miss the sensations and beauty of our own environment, and the thoughts and feelings you could be feeling in this exact moment.

Mindfulness involves being deliberately conscious about where your attention is focused. It's a choice you make.

It's about grabbing hold of those 'wandering thoughts' and focusing them on, right where you are at this moment.

It could be a project that you're working on, or listening to a lecture from a person. Maybe it's a dinner with friends or a day off from work.

Matt Killingsworth, a researcher at Harvard University, found that the average person's mind is wandering around and feeling unfocused for 47% of the day.

That's nearly half of our day!

When we're on "autopilot", we're allowing ourselves to become more vulnerable to feelings of stress, anxiety, or regret.

By thinking ahead to the future, you're probably thinking of the stressful situations that could occur, whether it's worrying about your rent being due, or how to get that job promotion.

When thinking about the past, you're often bombarded with feelings of regret or pain when you think of stressful events, like the death of a loved one or the break-up of a relationship.

It can be hard to separate yourself from those thoughts but it can mean better health, if you try and think only about what you're doing in the present moment.

Being mindful is about being engaged in what you're doing now, without any judgment. You simply want to react to your experiences as they occur, without getting caught up in the storm of emotional turmoil.

Think of it this way: it's like you're the audience watching a play. You don't want to get involved in what's happening on stage, but you're reacting to what you're seeing and feeling, and how the emotion of the moment affects you.

Mindfulness is similar! You don't want to rely on your old habits of how to think and feel.

You want to be open to new emotions and thoughts as they occur, without feeling like you're relying on your past experiences.

What is Meditation?

Meditation comes from the Latin root word 'meditatum', which means 'to ponder'.

The exact history of how meditation was created is unclear because many ancient civilizations had practices of repetitive chanting and staring at the fire in a trance-like state.

It's possible that they stumbled upon the beneficial properties of meditation, without even realizing it! Then they would pass on the knowledge from generation to generation.

The practice itself could be somewhere around 5,000 years old.

The Hindus originally used meditation as a way to draw deeper to the true nature of their God. That was the purpose that the original "Buddha", or a man by the name of Siddhartha Gautama, used meditation around 500 BCE.

Meditation soon spread into the Buddhist region of India, then further into Taoist China and Japan. It mostly stayed exclusively within Asia until the middle of the 20th century.

Why? Well, because travel was extremely hard in those days and passing on a tradition like this would require more explanation and teaching into the methods.

As travel between regions became easier, the practice of meditation became known in the West around the mid-20th century.

In 1958, Jack Kerouac published 'The Dharma Bums' to share his experiences exploring Buddhism and following the teachings of meditation. It was known as more of a "hippie" practice for many decades and a bunch of "hokey" that had actual medicinal affects.

Only in the 1960s and '70s did researchers begin to test meditation and learn more about its benefits in a scientific measure. 1979 is when the first trial research is believed to have been conducted in the United States, at the University of Massachusetts.

Jon Kabat-Zinn treated patients with chronic illness by using mindfulness and meditation techniques. He later went on to the found the Mindfulness-Based Stress Reduction program at the University.

The National Center for Complementary and Alternative Medicine published a study in 2007, that nearly 9.4% of Americans have meditated and continue to use meditation as a tool for physical and mental wellness. So much for "hokey" science!

The practice of yoga as meditation is believed to have originated in ancient India as well. As early as the 3rd millennium BCE there were seals and drawings, depicting figures in various stretching or meditation poses.

The split between Buddhism and Hinduism, regarding meditation, occurred because Hindus used meditation as a way to reach closer to their God, but Buddhists incorporated it into their daily life to gain mental clarity.

The traditional Abrahamic religions have some sort of meditation as well, whether it's devout daily prayers in Islam, or Eastern Christian meditation that includes repeating prayers and physical postures. These are a way to achieve a closer plane of spirituality when it comes to connecting with God and elevating your enlightenment.

In the late '90s and early 2000s in the West, yoga primarily became a popular exercise, as people became aware of its spiritual and medicinal benefits.

Whether it was prenatal yoga, or yoga classes for the elderly, this phenomenon of combining physical and mental health swept the nation. It was a way to stretch and exercise the body, but take some time to get away from the stress and anxiety of our lives. It provided exercise for the body and soul!

They can seem similar concepts but think of it more like nesting dolls. Meditation is a technique you can incorporate to lead a more mindful life.

Meditation doesn't mean clearing your mind, or getting rid of your thoughts, but being aware of the thoughts you have and not reacting to them negatively.

By grasping this technique, you can live a more mindful life where you are open and accepting of what is happening to you.

Mindfulness is a whole philosophy and a way of life, consciously making the decision to be aware of your emotions and how you react to stress you may encounter.

It involves many techniques, including meditation, as a way to train your mind to be more focused and positive.

3

THE PROBLEM WITH OUR LIVES

Even though the economy is booming, and average family income has increased, the truth is, our mental health as a society is suffering more than ever. When we look at the statistics, it's hard to believe how prevalent problems of mental health have spread.

A study in the Social Indicators Research Journal, that sampled nearly a total amount of 7 million people, found that 3 in 4 teenagers stated they had trouble sleeping.

50% of college students said they felt overwhelmed by their life. 20% of adults in the United States face a mental health problem.

Studies show that while mental illness and depression can occur at any age, it most often appears when people are in their mid-20s.

Women are nearly two times more likely than men to suffer from depression, with four times as many women committing suicide.

When we see these statistics, we can see how important mental health is, and that good mental health should as early as childhood.

Why is it that in today's society we hear so much about people being stressed or anxious about their life?

There are many theorized reasons and we will look at each one. But the simple matter is that we have become so busy in today's society, and we are overwhelmed by all the stimulants around us.

The average person has nearly 35,000 thoughts a day. That's a lot!

We have so many responsibilities in today's world, that we are stretched too thin to focus on ourselves.

Whether it's work, family, volunteering, our children's activities, school events, standardized tests, relationships... our mind is constantly moving and forcing us to think ahead.

We don't have or take the time to stop and invest in ourselves. As we divide our free time more and more to give to activities, we are forgetting to take time for ourselves.

Let me ask you a question.

Have you taken the time to unwind today, or even this week?

With the "go, go, go" routine of our lives, we can all too easily forget to take time to pause and focus on ourselves.

Today's world is one that measures success based on materialistic items. When it comes to worldly possessions, we're constantly told by advertisers that having the biggest house, luxury car, and designer handbag is going to make you 'cool' or 'successful'.

Advertising is everywhere to assault our senses. And with new forms of technology, forms of advertising have only shifted. Marketers get to us from everywhere - billboards, commercials, video games, social media ads, movie previews, subway ads, even the back of cereal boxes!

We're constantly being told what to buy, and how it'll improve our lives. And after we give in and buy something, then there's a new model out and advertisers are after us to get the upgrade!

A 2006 study by CBS found that in the 1970s people were exposed to nearly 500 ads a day. By 2006, that number was 5,000! But the truth is, putting a value on materialistic things like fame, money, and reputation has a positive correlation with depression and anxiety.

Dr. Tim Kasser wrote a book called *'The High Price of Materialism'* in 2002 which shed light on trends related to materialism. It showed the more value someone put on materialism, the less they valued intrinsic qualities like honesty, respectfulness and bravery. A higher value on materialistic qualities in life was linked to anxiety, mental illness, depression, and substance abuse.

Having more stuff does not make you happier! He urged readers to focus on having a life where they did something they enjoyed doing for work (even if it paid less!) and filled their time with people and causes they genuinely cared about.

Let's not forget how today's toxic consumption

of social media also has an impact on mental illness.

Today's society is becoming increasingly dependent on social media when it comes to things like maintaining friendships, getting movie or concert tickets, and even ordering groceries!

Sadly, social media and a limited view into someone's life can cause feelings of anxiety, insecurity, and envy. Most of us don't take the time to reflect on how social media affects us.

Do you feel envious when you see someone's new items? Do you feel jealous when you see someone with a significant other, on vacation, or buying a new house or car?

For people who are struggling financially or motivationally, these kinds of things can be triggering and cause feelings of sadness.

Of course, social media is great, to keep up with families and friends, but think about how it's affecting you and how you feel when you are browsing your feed.

If you're becoming consumed in other people's lives, instead of simply enjoying the connection with loved ones, then you are not being mindful about your own life.

A 2018 study published in the *Journal of Social & Clinical Psychology* compared two groups of undergraduate students at the University of Pennsylvania. One group continued using up to 3 social media platforms as usual, and the other group limited their use.

At the end of the trial period, researchers found that the group that limited their use had significantly les feelings of depression, loneliness, and insecurity.

Social media is supposed to make us feel *less* lonely, but it can often do the opposite.

It's important that in order to be mindful and more aware in our own lives, we have to realize we cannot dwell and obsess over the lives of others, especially people like celebrities or influencers.

Another trend in today's society, is that social media can often stop users from attending actual social gatherings and making relationships with people around them.

Despite the magic of the World Wide Web, in creating friendships with people all over the world, research shows that face-to-face contact is more important in reducing the risk of depression.

Oregon State University conducted a study of nearly 11,000 participants and found that, the ones who had little face-to-face contact, doubled their risk of having depression two years later.

The group that had physical contact with family or friends at least three times a week had less chance of having depression later in life.

It can become harder to socialize, the older you get, and the more people find a home in social media, the harder it can be for them to make connections in the world around them.

Previous generations tended also to have stronger family and kinship ties, such as the classic "dinner as a family" and "weekends at Grandma's house".

Nowadays, with people chasing opportunities around the globe and relocating away from family, it can be harder to maintain those ties and connections. Studies prove that people who receive more emotional support are better at dealing with signs of stress.

As our society becomes more consumed with materialism, and chasing after our goals, it can be hard to maintain those relationships that were so vital to us when we were young.

It's also true that the stigma of mental illness was more prevalent in previous decades, and many people may have suffered silently.

4

THE HEALTH BENEFITS OF MINDFULNESS AND MEDITATION

If you're just researching techniques of mindfulness and meditation, it can seem like a bunch of "hippie" nonsense to you.

But what about when we have the science to prove its beneficial effects on our health?

Scientific research studies prove that mindfulness can reduce feelings of stress, anxiety, depression, insomnia, and other feelings that can be linked to mental illness.

Stress

Mindfulness is proven to decrease feelings of stress that someone is experiencing.

Dr. Herbert Benson, a cardiologist at Harvard Medical School found that the stress hormone, called cortisol, can be reduced, when subjects practiced daily relaxation techniques.

Lower amounts of the stress hormone in the bloodstream can boost a person's overall mood and emotional wellbeing, and even help their immune system function better.

These relaxation techniques included things like breathing exercises, visualizing a tranquil, relaxing environment, prayer, or yoga.

But Dr. Benson's research showed that, in his trial group, where participants did relaxation techniques over eight weeks, the participants were able to reduce levels of blood pressure medication they were on.

Half of the group, that's 50%, were even able to eliminate one blood pressure medication. That's significantly higher than in the control group, where only 19% eliminated their medication.

Depression

In order to ease some of the symptoms of depression, you'll be surprised to know that exercises of mindfulness can help with that too!

Where does the idea for this come from? It seems that Buddhist monks who practiced meditation and mindfulness nearly 3,000 years ago were on to something.

Oxford University's Department of Psychiatry conducted an experiment, in 2009, on groups of patients who had experienced periods of depression and battled suicidal thoughts.

They found that the group that practiced mindfulness, along with their usual treatment of medication, reported their symptoms decreased from "severe" to "mild" levels of depressing thoughts. The group that did not practice mindfulness had no significant change in their thoughts.

To add to these results, Dr. Zindel V. Segal published a study in 2010 that found patients in remission from depression, who lived a mindful approach of their life, were less likely to relapse than patients jut on remission with the help of medication.

This is amazing research to show how a little time to reflect and view the world differently can have a big impact on your life.

Insomnia

Insomnia, or an inability to sleep, is another condition that can affect people who live with depression or are battling stressful scenarios. At the end of the day when you're laying exhausted in bed, your brain should be able to turn off all your thoughts to give you a good night's sleep and regenerate for tomorrow. However, if our brains are overloaded, we remain on alert and are unable to fall asleep.

Mindfulness is a great technique to help cure insomnia.

At the Mindful Awareness Research Center at the University of California, Los Angeles (UCLA), researchers found that mindfulness can actually increase a person's sense of calm and regulate their stress to result in a better night's sleep.

Yes, it really does all come back to stress as the culprit.

Stress is what keeps you awake at night and keeps those thoughts running through your head even when you desperately need sleep.

A study at the Minnesota Academic Health Center in 2009 found that people who successfully went through a mindfulness program, geared to reduce stress factors in their life, decreased the effects of their chronic insomnia, equivalent to a group that went on medicine to help them sleep.

That's the same improvement, without taking any drugs.

They practiced being more mindful of their life and reacting better to any stress that they were experiencing. The participants stated they fell asleep more quickly and felt they slept longer and better - without any side effects!

Instead, listening to some guided mentation and practicing breathing exercises could be just what you need to unwind after a long day and lull your body into sleep.

Mindfulness can even improve cognitive function! Things like working memory, and focus, improved in participants when they incorporated sessions of mindfulness or meditation in their routine.

It can improve your efficiency with things like work or school, and allow you to be more clear-headed and focused.

A 2018 study at Osnabrück University in Germany divided participants into two groups: one that practiced mindful meditation and another group that did muscle relaxation exercises.

At the end of the trial period, researchers found that the group that meditated had a 10% positive significant change in their working memory and cognitive exercises. The numbers didn't change at all for the participants in the control group.

These results indicated an increase of productivity, as you're able to focus more intently on tasks, and have a higher level of cognitive function to achieve them. That's a smart side-effect!

Another piece of research on brain activity, related to meditation, comes from studies conducted with an EEG, or an electroencephalogram. This machine gives a depiction of the brain's electrical activity when a person is directed to complete a certain task or think of something in particular.

An overwhelming amount of research has found that participants who meditated tended to have their SSVEP brain signals decreased by nearly 70%. These are the continuous brain signals the body sends when you need to complete a task.

The reduction in brain activity means that fewer brain resources are actually needed to complete the task. By adding meditation and mindfulness to your day, you're minimizing your stress and improving your cognitive function.

One of the biggest findings though, is that mindfulness can improve the quality of your marriage.

Research at the University of North Carolina at Chapel Hill, in 2004, found that a group of participants who practiced mindfulness, had a correlation of more consecutive days of happiness in their relationship.

Practicing mindfulness more positively impacted couples' levels of satisfaction in their relationship, closeness and acceptance of one another, and decreased their relationship stress. Sounds like just what any marriage needs - a good dose of mindfulness, to get you back into the honeymoon phase.

With results like these, it's easy to see why mindfulness has such a positive impact in the relationships around you.

As your stress and anxiety levels decrease, you're able to be more generous and present in the people around you and focus on them for a change.

It's an important factor that to change the way your relationships are functioning, you have to take some time to work on yourself first.

External stress never goes away, but if you're more mindful about how you react to what's happening around you, you can achieve better mental health.

Mindfulness encourages the body to feel at peace with ourselves and our current scenario, instead of focusing on an overwhelming and complex world.

5

PRACTICAL GUIDE TO MEDITATION TECHNIQUES

We've talked about how meditation can really impact your life positively.

Many of us may associate meditation with the saying of a mantra, or with Eastern traditions. However, meditation is an ancient spiritual discipline that has been practiced for centuries, across different religions.

Let's explores ways that you can incorporate it into your everyday life.

Walking Meditation

Guided walking meditation is a way for you to get both physical exercise and improve your mental wellbeing.

A 2004 study, in the *Journal for Psychosomatic Research*, found that in an eight-week program with participants, those that took part in walking meditation, reported an improvement in their psychological wellbeing.

Its aim is more than just a pleasant walk around the neighborhood. The goal is to increase your awareness of external and internal surroundings, and tune into the experiences and scenery we often miss in the journey to our destination.

By paying more attention to the world around us, we can appreciate it more.

To begin, find a location that gives you ample space to walk back and forth for a good 15 to 20 paces. It can be indoors or outdoors, but a good amount of space, so that you're not constrained.

Start your steps slowly and then pause for breath as you go. It may sound silly to break down the steps of walking even further, but the point of meditation is to be aware of every moment and make it purposeful.

That purposefulness begins with lifting your foot and moving it forward from where you're standing, and then placing it on the ground, and shifting your weight, and then your other foot touching the ground. The cycle continues, back and forth.

Focus your attention on the things you normally wouldn't, like the movement of your feet and legs, how the ground feels against your shoes, the way your body is held, and the sound and views around you.

When your mind wanders, try and focus it again, on one of these sensations, so you can keep your mind focussed on what's around you in this present moment.

Visualization Meditation

This is a powerful technique to use the mind to empower us with a vision of our desired outcomes. This allows for our attention on our goals to grow stronger, and the outside distractions to grow weaker. The unconscious mind is very powerful and this hopes to harness that energy and turn into reality.

First, identify your desired outcome. Whether it's attaining physical health or reaching a goal for yourself.

Think about what would make you feel at peace and what emotions you would feel.

Do you see your body as healthy and strong? Do you see your relationship with a loved one to be repaired and the fractures fixed?

Create a vision of what that would look like.

Imagine the sounds and the look. Imagine how you would feel in that moment and in that reality.

Enter into a state of meditation as you relax, and take deep breaths, and surround yourself with that image you have created.

Immerse yourself into that vision as if it's already happening and you're living in it, that you're surrounded by those feelings and sensations and the joy of it.

When it's time to leave the state of meditation, slowly allow the image to fade away.

This sort of positive visualization method is encouraged at least once a day, for 10 to 15 minutes, to keep a person motivated in reaching their goals.

Active Gaze Meditation

This is where you focus your thoughts on something specific, to guide your thoughts to only one thing at a time.

Your mind will probably wander, until you get used to this method. Try to be aware of when your thoughts have drifted and quickly "snap back" your mental focus to the present.

Set aside a few minutes each day when you have time to meditate. Sit with good posture, or you can sit cross-legged or in a chair if that's a more comfortable position for you.

Now, it's time to focus your gaze at a simple object near you, like a word written on a piece of paper, or the flame of a candle.

Force away thoughts intruding into your mind, and focus on keeping a "clean slate" mind as you gaze at the object. Those thoughts will intrude, but it's about forcing yourself not to react to each thought as it hits you.

You want to keep your calm and keep your focus on the object in front of you. As your meditation time ends, take deep breaths from your abdomen, as you break your gaze with the object.

Mantra Meditation

Mantra comes from the Hindu language and means "word". Some spiritual meditation teachers use this type of meditation to mean that it has the power to convey "secret" words to the soul and gain enlightenment.

Words have power.

For example, how do you feel when you repeat the word "anger" over and over again? You start to suddenly …. feel angry and your hands might become clenched and your heart begins to race.

Now, try repeating the word "love". You'll instantly know how your body changes in response to this new word.

The word initiates feeling within you. This will give you an idea of how mantra meditation works.

You can enter a meditation trance using any simple words or phrases that you find relaxing or calming.

You might prefer to use a saying like, "I am ___".

Fill in the sentence with your goal and how you want to feel that day. "I am going to have a great day." "I am smart and successful at my job." "I am blessed to have today."

Using such mantras to meditate is a great manifestation technique. It allows the mind to visualize a feeling or goal, so that your body loses resistance to it and accepts the vision it sees as the future.

Christian Meditation

Faith-based meditation is about connecting with God. It's about becoming mindful of God and His Word.

Although some might throw their hands up in horror at the words 'Christian' and 'meditation' being seen together, meditation and contemplation have had a place for hundreds of years in Christian tradition.

The Hebrew word for meditation, itself means to 'recite softly'. Repetition can be powerful. Consider reading or reciting softly the words from a favorite Psalm, hymn or Bible verse.

You may find it easier to use a mantra. If so, try saying the word 'maranatha', which means, 'The Lord is coming' or 'Come Lord'.

Another way of Christian meditation, is to read a Bible passage and then to visualise yourself inside the story. Picture the scene, the people around you, imagining yourself into the story that you have been reading about.

The beauty of Christian meditation is that you

can focus on a single word or phrase, that jump out to your from the pages of the Bible.

Focus on a word or phrase, and repeat it to yourself, internalising it's meaning. If you find your mind wandering, just bring it back to focusing on the word or phrase.

Meditation stills the mind, focuses the mind away from anxious thoughts and can help us connect with God.

Yoga Meditation

Yoga also dates back to roots in ancient India. There are many styles and practices of it but they all involve taking part in controlled breathing exercises and a series of stretches to promote flexibility and calm your thoughts.

Each posture requires concentration and balance, as you clear your mind and focus all your energy on holding the position and following the breathing ritual. All of that coupled with relaxation allows you to stay immersed in the moment and enjoy the exercise, and to experience the sensation of the stretching muscles in your body.

The idea of the yoga poses is to create strength and flexibility, and to be aware of your body in a greater sense. While stretching, you're testing your body's limbs and pushing boundaries as you hold new positions. It's a way to focus on your body and push the limits of what it can do, and how far it can stretch.

When first starting yoga, beginners may notice that they're struggling with doing the simplest stretches and having trouble even touching their toes.

The beauty of yoga is, just like with other exercises and activities, practice makes perfect. The more you try to achieve these new limits and stretches, the more flexible you will ultimately become.

The meditation aspect of yoga has been proven to lower stress and anxiety, reduce high blood pressure, and even help manage chronic pain conditions.

With many different types of stretches and activity levels, yoga has been split into many factions: for seniors, for pregnant women, for the chronically ill.

Yoga can be a great way to exercise both the mind and spirit.

6

A GUIDE TO MINDFULNESS TECHNIQUES

Mindfulness is the buzz word of the day, but how can we incorporate mindfulness into our busy everyday lives?

Here's some ways that you can start to begin to practice mindfulness in your life.

Practice Mindful Driving

Distracted driving results in nearly 9 deaths in the United States every day, not to mention more than 1,000 people injured because of this carelessness.

With today's need for constant social media fix and texting, the more distracted you are, the more damage you can cause on the road. When you're visually and manually distracted when driving a vehicle, it can increase your risk of causing or getting in an accident.

By practicing mindful driving, you want to be alert every step of the way to your destination. Driving can cause feelings of stress and anxiety in some people, not to mention the road rage that occurs when it's a long commute, and traffic or construction is involved.

When you get into your car, take a few deep breaths before you begin. Turn off the radio, if it's a distraction for you, or maybe you prefer having some soothing background music.

Turn your phone to silent or automated out loud messages so that way, if someone sends an urgent message, the auto-speak can read it out to you.

As you begin driving your usual route, take the time to be aware of your surroundings. Look at the people and the places around you, not to mention any traffic signs that you may have previously missed!

If someone cuts you off or you get stuck in traffic, notice the feelings that arise in you. Practice some deep, calming breaths, when you are a traffic light or waiting for a turn.

When you arrive at your destination, take a second to sit and take deep breaths. Let go on the exhalation and allow yourself to be aware of your new surroundings, before you exit your vehicle.

Relaxation Technique for Insomnia

Find a quiet and peaceful place where you can sit for about 10 to 15 minutes. Dim the lights, be sure there are no distractions, like your phone or a TV screen, and take some time to settle your thoughts mentally and sit still physically.

Find somewhere you can sit up straight in an upright position. Use a stool or a pillow to keep yourself comfortable, but be sure you're in the right posture and not slouching.

Notice if any part of your body is tense and take some breaths to ease the tension out of your body. Take three deep breaths in, three deep breaths out.

Focus your attention to the tip of your nose. Notice how you are feeling warm when exhaling and cool when inhaling, and how that sensation feels.

As you breath in and exhale, let the warmth of

exhaling and cool of inhaling be your thoughts for the next five minutes.

Take deep breaths and be aware of the air that is moving through your body - from your nostrils down to your throat and into your lungs. Then back out, from your lungs, to your throat to your nostrils. Follow the passage your breath, in and out, in and out.

Even if you are getting distracted by other thoughts, focus on your breathing and continue your meditation. Each time you find yourself distracted, bring your focus back to your breathing.

When you're ready to complete the breathing technique, take three deep breaths from your stomach and rest your weight against the chair. Then, begin to stretch your body and open your eyes, as you adjust back to your surroundings.

Practice the Pomodoro Technique

Pomodoro is a work technique to mindfully focus your time on one task and increase overall productivity. It's easy to incorporate into your working day and has been proven to be effective.

Often our mind is scattered. We're busy thinking of the things we need to do.

Even when we're working on one assignment, we're thinking about ideas for the next one, wondering if we should be working on that instead!

The Pomodoro technique allows you to immerse yourself fully in the one assignment you're working on, to increase your mental focus.

You'll work on one thing and one thing alone. After that, you can take a break and work on something else!

First, decide by urgency, which task needs to be worked on first. Set your timer to 25 minutes.

If you're using your phone timer, you're at least placing it across the room so it won't become a distraction. Work on the one task at hand diligently, until the timer rings. Record the task as completed and take a short 5 minute break.

Work through at least four Pomodoro time blocks and you can treat yourself to a longer 15 to 20 minute break.

This technique is all about staying focused on one task. It allows you to make significant progress on it and then move on to the next one.

By being mindful about where your attention is focused, you really can get more done!

Work on Mundane Tasks, Mindfully

It can sound funny, but doing mundane, repetitive, "boring" tasks like washing dishes, vacuuming, or sweeping can actually decrease your stress levels, if done mindfully!

These little chores are a great way to "turn off" your brain from the stress-filled thoughts that might be occupying it.

Doing a task, like washing the dishes by hand or organizing a cluttered bookshelf, can help you appreciate the more simple pleasures in your life.

You allow your mind to be focused on the repetitive task in front of you: like not dropping the dishes in soapy water and organizing the books in an aesthetically pleasing pattern.

It's a great way to shut off your mind for a little while. Don't worry, this doesn't mean you should wash the dishes by hand every night. But occasionally, taking part in a repetitive task like this, can give you some quiet time to yourself.

Try Adult Coloring Books

It may sound silly at first, but adult coloring books have become a national phenomenon recently for a reason!

They have therapeutic benefits and can decrease a person's anxiety, tension, and stress levels.

It's a way to practice mindfulness because it requires your full focus, as you slow down and think about what you're working on and color away!

It's almost like a mini-meditation session, because your thoughts float away and all you're worried about is coloring within the lines.

Coloring is an activity that's unique, because it gives a full brain workout. It's not just a "right" brain or a "left" brain activity.

It involves creativity with picking color choices and deciding on an aesthetic picture, but it also utilizes the frontal lobe of the brain to concentrate and focus on the spatial organization of a picture. There's also the use of fine motor skills to make precise movements.

It's a way for the entire brain to be fully occupied and truly block out any external noise.

Have you noticed that sometimes when people are concentrating on coloring, it's almost like they're under hypnosis? Like they're in some sort of trance? Well, that's because they're completely focused on the task at hand!

It might be worth trying colouring. It's relaxing, it's calming, and it allows your mind to unwind from the stressors of a long day.

Practice Mindful Eating

Some people believe mindful eating can be associated with weight loss, but that's not it at all.

In fact, it's about slowing down and enjoying your food, being completely aware of how it tastes, and paying attention to the flavors of it.

Most of the time we're eating semiconsciously, just going through the motions, without even realizing how much we're eating or what our food tastes like.

How many meals do we eat while we're "multitasking" on our phone? Or in front of the TV, as we are distracted by what's onscreen?

We're not aware of what's in front of us, we're merely shovelling food in our mouth to satisfy our hunger and move on to the next task of our day.

Eating like this, often results in overeating, and it causes you to miss out on the delicious, sensory pleasure of enjoying your meals.

Being mindful about your food can also stop you from having an unhealthy relationship with it, such as overeating, binging, or alcoholism.

Think about how you feel when having a Thanksgiving or Christmas dinner with family, versus how you eat at home.

Doesn't putting your phones away, enjoying every bite of food and the company you have, make it much more special?

Why not associate that practice into your daily meals? Sure, maybe breakfast and lunch are hectic for you, but try being mindful with your dinner.

Don't have any distractions nearby and enjoy slowly eating your food and enjoying every sensation. Whether it's salty, sour, spicy, or sweet!

By being aware of what you're eating, and how you feel after every bite, you might cut back on your portion size when you realize you feel full already!

Mindful Listening

Mindfulness listening encourages you to use your auditory sense in a non-judgmental way with the world around you.

Maybe there are sounds you've been tuning out, whether it's just traffic or your noisy neighbors, or the music on the subway during your morning commute.

Sometimes we're so busy and consumed with our thoughts, we don't realize the noises of the world around us! Often we're listening to a song on the radio and nodding along to the words, without even listening to the music!

For this exercise, put on your headphones and choose a piece of music that you've never heard before. Don't judge the music by its name or artist, and ignore any reviews you may have heard.

This is all about you, experiencing the song for the first time. Explore every part of the song: the tempo, lyrics, beat, chorus, range, tone and rhythm. Allow your entire body to be consumed by it, so you feel like you are surrounded by the sound waves.

Try and separate each sound individually in your mind, so you can appreciate each one. Especially if there's more than one instrument in a classical piece or more than one voice in a song.

Try and appreciate each vocal or instrumental note as individual pieces of a larger composition.

The idea is to listen to something intently and carefully, without any judgment or preconception. You want the music to consume you, so you can say you've listened to the song without any distraction.

Beyond music, try and incorporate mindful listening in your daily life.

How often is it that you sit out on your balcony and simply listen to the sounds of the city? Often we're multi-tasking and on our phone and finishing work for the office.

When was the last time you simply sat there and listened to the sounds around you?

Mindful listening is a great way to focus on the largeness of life and get a sense of perspective, realizing how significantly tiny we are in the grand scheme of things.

Mindful Appreciation

This is a technique much like an appreciation journal or keeping a diary of things you're grateful for.

In our busy lives, we simply don't take enough time to appreciate the insignificant things, that assist us in our survival.

We're too busy chasing after bigger dreams, like houses and salaries or promotions, to ponder over the little things that help us on a day-to-day scale. Little things like electricity, clean clothes, clean drinking water, having your sight and your sense of smell, and being able to see the world around you.

We are so busy thinking about the "big" things in our life, that we don't take enough time to ponder the little things. We don't process about how we are so lucky to have these things, or acknowledge how much they help our life and benefit us.

Compare yourself who may have ailing health, or people in impoverished countries who don't have the same basic safety or living conditions that you do.

Take some time when you meditate to jot down 5 things that you appreciate and that are gifts in your life. Try to make them more minute things that you might not think about on a daily basis.

The point of this exercise is simply to give thanks and be more open to the little things in our life that we overlook.

Conclusion

We've looked at seven different techniques,

- mindful driving
- relaxation techniques for insomnia
- the Pomodoro technique
- working on mundane tasks
- focused coloring
- mindful eating and
- mindful listening

To start incorporating mindfulness into your life, which of these techniques will you start to apply in the next week?

By making a start in the next week, you're one step closer to making mindfulness a habit in your daily life.

7

THE POWER OF MINDFULNESS AND MEDITATION

When learning a new skill, the brain adjusts and begins to adapt to what it's taught.

It's called neuroplasticity, or the brain's ability to make new connections, as you introduce new skills. It happens when people learn new languages or learn a new form of martial arts.

The brain reacts to what we do, but also how we think and feel. That's why living a life of mindfulness is so important.

The more you practice being aware of your life and being more present in your day to day activities and thoughts, the more your brain adjusts to this lifestyle, and makes it a permanent way of life for you.

As they say, the first step is the hardest. The beautiful thing about meditation is that you don't need to be practicing for years, in order to see results.

Studies have shown that even just 8 weeks of regular meditation can transform the connections in the brain! In that short time span, many studies have found that patients reported less anxiety, stress, and signs of depression.

With improvements in your mental health, you're able to react to everyday life with more calm and awareness.

Mindfulness is the practice of being more aware of the moment you're in. This allows you to savor your experiences and the people you are spending your time with.

So much of our day passes so quickly, and if you aren't aware of what you're doing and enjoying the experience, you've wasted the time.

When we focus our mind completely on where we are and what we're are doing, the world and its experiences open up, and we're able to completely take in our surroundings and the world's beauty.

It's all about the experience, not the judgment or any preconceived notions.

Even when you're having a meal, how much of your food do you enjoy and savor? Or are you in a rush to finish your meal and have the TV on as a distraction?

By slowing down your life and taking the time to enjoy your meal and savor each food, you'll become more appreciative and thankful in general.

There's an example in mindfulness, about burned toast.

Let's say you burn a piece of toast when making your breakfast. How do you react to it?

Do you end up cranky and agonizing that you should have gotten to it a minute earlier and salvaged the slice?

Perhaps you anxiously keep watch over the next piece, to ensure it doesn't end up the same way? Or do you simply toss it out and continue on with your day?

Mindfulness is about being present in the moment, about seizing each moment as its own, and not allowing the past or present or dictate it.

Often we find ourselves preoccupied with the past or the present. Whether it's past regrets or future worries, we're dividing ourselves between the past or the future, without allowing ourselves to fully experience the present, today.

Mindfulness urges us to occupy ourselves with this moment. Mindfulness is about living life, moment to moment, free from thoughts of the past or anxieties about the future.

When are you able to be more fully present in your experiences, you are able to take in the world around you.

It's like, if you went on a vacation to a tropical island. Wouldn't you want to take the time to enjoy the view and the sights and the sounds around you?

You don't want to waste that valuable time worrying about the work you left back home, or how you're going to pay for dinner. You want to enjoy the experience, before it's gone.

Mindfulness urges you to be more aware of your surroundings and the beauty in them. The more you see life as this current moment, the more kind and loving you can be towards yourself and others.

When you see the science behind meditation, and how it improves mental and physical health, it seems like a great motivation to incorporate some of this activity into your day.

Even if it's just 10 or 15 minutes before bed, it can greatly improve the quality of your sleep. By finding a quiet, comfortable spot and taking some time to gather your thoughts, and be focused on a mantra or visualization of your future success, you can organize your feelings and better equip yourself for tomorrow.

In fact, meditation improves brain function and allows you to be more focused. Think of focus like a muscle that needs to be given a workout.

Just like you'd take your body to the gym, to get in shape, the more you practice on focusing your attention, the less divided your thoughts will be during your normal day.

You'll find you can get more done and your thoughts aren't scrambled.

In a world where we're so fast-paced and have less and less human interaction, it can be hard to feel empathetic.

Research has shown that meditation is positively linked with creativity in artists.

Meditation can even make you a kinder person.

A 2008 study found that people who meditated regularly had more active levels in their temporal brain, which is tied to empathy.

When they heard the sounds of people suffering, they reacted more empathetically, than the control group of people, who didn't meditate.

In a world that is constantly changing and in turmoil, isn't it a beautiful thing to know that we can teach ourselves to be more kind to one another?

8

GETTING STARTED

Your life is busy. Really busy.

So, how are you going to make a start on reducing the stressors in your life, by incorporating mindfulness and meditation?

Here are some tips to get yourself going.

Find the time

The truth is, your life is busy and it's always going to be.

Unless you're serious about meditation and becoming a more mindful person, the time won't magically appear in your schedule, until you carve a place for it!

You have to decide that meditation is important enough for you to stop doing everything else and focus on it and *only* it!

To find the time, consider adding your 'meditation' time to your diary or calendar, blocking out that time, so that it's a fixed time in your day or week.

Make it a part of your routine

Meditation only works if you make time for it and ensure it has a place in your day.

Whether it's in the morning, after you wake up, a quick break at lunch, or some quiet time before bed - you need to prioritise your physical and mental wellbeing.

People who rush through their busy day and don't make time to unwind, or take a moment to themselves, often have trouble sleeping.

Make it a habit to have meditation as a part of your day, so that you're not going without it.

You have a schedule in your life for other things - your meals, your meetings, waking up, and going to sleep. So make sure you make a place for meditation too!

Use a meditation app to help you meditate wherever you are

Whether it's a few quick minutes in your office during the day, or time on your morning or evening commute, meditation apps have made it convenient and comfortable for you to fit meditation into your day, no matter where you are.

You can also download some great meditations as audiobooks on Amazon, Audible or iTunes.

This is a great way to have the opportunity to meditate, right at your fingertips. Now, you just have to make the time in your busy day!

When you find some quiet time, put in your headphones, or turn up the volume and your app and let your mind drift away.

Practice mindfulness whenever you can

Some people think of mindfulness as an "all or none" formula.

The truth is, we're busy people and our lives can be filled with roles and responsibilities. It can be hard to guide yourself to living a mindful life, all at once. So take the time to incorporate it, when you can!

Whether it's taking the time to be mindful when you're eating lunch, or taking a quick walk around the block on your lunch break, to clear your head and prepare for the rest of the day.

Maybe, you can use your time between classes to do some breathing exercises to calm your anxiety. Or maybe it's putting away your phone before bed and taking time to write in your journal.

Even finding the time for one activity a day is better for your overall health than skipping it entirely.

Keep a designated seat or cushion for meditation

It may sound silly, but the truth is, your brain associates something familiar with the activity you use it for.

So, when you are meditating, try and keep the routine with one blanket, or one chair, or one cushion that you find comfortable.

Your mind will come to associate it with the feelings of positivity and relaxation that meditation gives you.

That forms a positive, emotional attachment between you and the object, and with you and meditation in general.

Create a mantra or phrase that fills you with positivity

Choose a phrase or mantra that helps you feel positive. Here's some examples, you might want to use:

- Relax. You're going to have a great day.
- I am here, I am present.
- I can face whatever the day brings me.
- You are a survivor.

Whatever your phrase is, allow it to be one that fills you with positivity and confidence, when you surround yourself with those uplifting words.

As you say them, focus on the words. Focus on how they make you feel, and what they indicate about the type of day or experience you will have.

Change up your meditation styles if you get bored

If you find yourself getting bored or dispassionate about your meditation style, whether it's gaze meditation or repeating a mantra, don't be scared to switch it up and try something new.

Sometimes your mind needs to be challenged and you might feel more comfortable trying something new, if your mind has become resistant to one type.

Allow yourself to try new experiences of meditation, whether it's yoga, journaling, or visualization methods.

Have a friend to keep tabs on you

Meditation itself is obviously an individual kind of activity. It's important that you feel like someone is with you on the journey and that you're not alone.

We urge you to have a friend who supports you in your journey for mental tranquility or holds you accountable. It can be encouraging and motivating to have someone like-minded at your side.

That could include going for yoga classes together, or simply checking in with each other during the day, to encourage each other to take a few minutes to meditate.

Always see it in a positive light

If you see any activity as a chore, chances are you'll come to dread it.

After learning about the beneficial health effects of meditation, you should see it as a positive activity. If you see it as such, you'll be more enthusiastic about making time to meditate and finding a place for it in your day.

If you begin to see it as a something to "get over with" and move on to the next task, you will not reap the full benefits of it.

Meditation is about taking time for you, it's all about you.

Approach it with a positive attitude and trust the science that says it will help you, and you can begin to reduce the stress and anxiety in your life.

9

CONCLUSION

If you're still wavering or wondering where to start, the easiest way to begin to incorporate meditation into your life, is to read or listen to a guided meditation.

We've included some links to relaxing meditations in the final chapter.

Still unsure? Why not revisit chapters five and six again, to see how you can easily incorporate meditation and mindfulness into your daily life.

Medical studies have shown us the benefits of mindfulness and meditation. If you incorporate them in your life, you'll start to feel the benefits of a quieter mind.

Your mental and physical health will benefit and you'll be better placed to manage your stress and anxiety levels.

You deserve to live a better life.

Why wait. Why not make a start today?

10

ONE MORE THING

If you've enjoyed this book, please consider leaving a rating or review.

11

MINDFULNESS MEDITATIONS

You can download these guided and listen to these guided meditations to help you practice mindfulness and meditation any place, any time.

Guided Meditation Audiobook Bundle

This bundle includes:

- *Mindfulness and Meditation for Beginners*
- *10 Minute Meditation*
- *Guided Meditation for Anxiety, Stress Relief and a Quiet Mind*
- *Guided Meditation for Sleep and Relaxation; Letting Go of Fear, Anxiety, and Worry*

- *Guided Meditation for Beginners* - for sleep, relaxation, anxiety and stress reduction
- *Letting Go - a Guided Meditation for Beginners for Mindfulness, Inner Peace, Stress Relief and Sleep*
- and a bonus track, *Guided Meditation Train Journey.*

These guided meditations can help you relax and calm your mind.

Each meditation is designed to be accompanied by relaxing music and read in a soothing voice to provide a calming meditation that helps you feel settled and at peace.

https://adbl.co/2KsNCqf

If you're not already an Audible listener, you can download your first meditation for free, by typing in the link above.

www.ingramcontent.com/pod-product-compliance
Lightning Source LLC
Chambersburg PA
CBHW071319080526
44587CB00018B/3278